CONTENTS

Words that look like this are explained
in the glossary on page 31.

THE ANIMAL KINGDOM

The animal kingdom includes over 1 million known living <u>species</u>. They come in many different shapes and sizes, they each do weird and wonderful things and they live all over planet Earth.

From the freezing Arctic waters to the hottest desert in the world, animals have <u>adapted</u> to the often extreme and diverse conditions on Earth.

Even though each and every species of animal is <u>unique</u>, they still share certain characteristics with each other. These shared characteristics are used to classify animals. There are six main groups used to classify animals. They are: mammals, reptiles, birds, insects, amphibians and fish.

Around **10,000 new** species of animal are discovered **every year**.

Birds include penguins, ducks, ostriches and owls.

BIRDS

WHAT IS A BIRD?

A bird is a type of animal that lays hard-shelled eggs and has a backbone, feathers and a hard beak.

All birds have wings and most birds use them to fly. However, some species of bird are flightless, meaning that they cannot fly. Birds are warm-blooded animals, which means that they maintain a stable body temperature, even if they live in a very hot or very cold <u>habitat</u>.

Flightless birds include ostriches, emus and penguins.

There are around 10,000 known species of bird alive today. Birds can come in many different shapes and sizes and each species has their own individual features that help them to survive in their habitats.

The largest bird on Earth is the ostrich, which stands at around 2.7 metres tall. The bee hummingbird is the smallest bird on Earth at around 5 centimetres (cm) long.

Ostrich

Bee hummingbird

Owls, eagles, chickens and peacocks are all types of bird.

BIRD CHECKLIST

- Lay hard-shelled eggs
- Have wings, feathers and beaks
- Most can fly
- Warm-blooded
- <u>Vertebrate</u>

BODY PARTS

Different species of bird can look very different from one another. However, there are some body parts that all birds have. We use these common traits to decide which animals are birds and which are not. All birds have a light skeleton, two wings, two legs, a beak and feathers all over their body. Also, birds always lay eggs instead of giving birth to live young.

Feathers

Two wings

Light skeleton

Beak

Two legs

BEAK

All birds have beaks; however, the shape and size of a bird's beak often depends on what it eats. If two birds have very different beaks, it probably means that they eat different foods or that they eat in different ways.

The pelican has a long beak with a large throat pouch. It scoops fish out of the sea using its beak and then drains any excess water out of its mouth using its throat pouch.

Pelican

Throat pouch

Woodpeckers have short, strong beaks that they use to drill through the bark on trees. This allows them to eat tree sap and insects that burrow into the bark.

Woodpecker

LEGS AND FEET

Birds always have two legs and two feet, with most species having four toes on each foot. However, not all bird feet are the same, as different species of bird have developed differently shaped feet depending on what they use them for.

Ducks have webbed feet, meaning that a thin layer of skin stretches between each of their toes. This helps them to swim faster.

Webbed feet

Owls have long and sharp claws, called talons, that make it easier for them to catch mice and frogs.

Talons

FEATHERS

Most birds are almost completely covered in feathers. While individual feathers are very thin, when feathers are packed close together they form a warm, waterproof layer. Birds can push their feathers closer together when the weather is cold or wet so that they stay warm and their skin stays dry. The colour of a bird's feathers can also be very important. The males of some bird species, such as the mandarin duck, use their colourful feathers to attract female birds of the same species.

Swans often have over 24,000 feathers, which is more than most other species of bird.

Mandarin duck

GETTING AROUND

Most birds get around by using their wings to fly. Birds need to have very light bodies or very large wings so that when they flap their wings they create enough <u>lift</u> to fly.

Small birds, such as robins, don't need big wings because they are so light. They only need a tiny amount of lift to keep them flying.

Robin

The wandering albatross has a <u>wingspan</u> of over three metres, which is larger than any other bird on the planet. Its wings are so big that it can often create enough lift to fly without having to flap — it can just glide along.

Wandering albatross

BREATHING

Birds breathe in their own unique way. Birds have two lungs but their lungs cannot squeeze or stretch to pull and push the air in and out of their bodies. Instead, birds have <u>organs</u> called air sacs.

Muscles around the air sacs can squeeze them to push air out of a bird's body. This is a better way to breathe than just using lungs as more <u>oxygen</u> is absorbed into the body with each breath.

Birds have between seven and eleven air sacs in their bodies, depending on what species they are.

PREDATORS AND PREY

All animals can be sorted into groups depending on what they eat. The three groups are carnivores, herbivores and omnivores.

Herbivores
Plant-eaters

Carnivores
Meat-eaters

Omnivores
Plant- and meat-eaters

An animal's teeth are usually shaped in a way that helps them to eat the food that makes up their diet. Birds don't have teeth but their beaks are often different depending on what they eat. Birds that are carnivores, such as vultures, usually have sharp beaks so that they can tear off pieces of meat more easily. Parakeets, which are herbivores, have short, hard beaks that are better at breaking up seeds and nuts.

Animals that hunt other animals are called predators, while animals that are hunted by other animals are called prey.

Birds that are predators are called raptors. Possibly the best raptor of them all is the bald eagle. The bald eagle is such a good predator because it has amazing eyesight and can swoop down on its prey at 160 kilometres per hour (kph).

The bald eagle is the national bird of the US.

Birds that are prey often live in groups and are usually slow at taking off, such as chickens and ducks. These birds make easy targets for land-based predators, such as foxes and cats.

CLIFFS, CAVES AND COASTLINES

Lots of birds live on cliffs near to the sea. Birds live in this habitat because it stops any predators from reaching them or their chicks. Living close to the sea is also an advantage because many of these birds mostly eat fish.

Puffins often live on cliffs near to the coast. These birds mainly eat a diet of fish and have wings that are adapted for swimming as well as flying. Living on the cliffs means that they can easily find food and stay safe from predators.

Puffins are able to swim to depths of 60 metres.

16

Birds sometimes live in caves to stay safe from predators. However, living in dark caves is a lot more difficult than living on cliffs, so these birds have had to adapt to survive.

Oilbirds live in large groups inside caves. Many of these caves are always dark inside, meaning that the oilbirds can't see anything. Oilbirds get around this by making high-pitched noises and then listening to how the sound echoes in the cave. Oilbirds have an amazing sense of hearing and can work out their surroundings by listening to the echoes. This method of seeing in the dark is called echolocation.

Oilbird

ADAPTATION

Birds have adapted to their environments in many amazing ways in order to survive.

The rock pigeon often travels far away from its nest to look for food. No matter how far they travel, rock pigeons can nearly always find their way home. Other animals often use the position of the Sun in the sky to show them the way home, but rock pigeons have adapted to use the <u>magnetic field</u> of the Earth as a guide instead.

Before advanced technology, rock pigeons were used to send messages all over the world because of their amazing ability to use the Earth's magnetic field.

Even though all birds have wings, not all birds can fly. Some birds that can't fly have adapted to use their wings in unique and amazing ways.

Ostriches can run so fast that they sometimes have to use their wings in order to slow themselves down and to help them to change direction.

Ostriches can run at around 65 kph.

The wings of penguins have adapted over time to help them to swim rather than fly. Having flipper-like wings mean that penguins can swim underwater at very high speeds.

LIFE CYCLES

A life cycle is the series of changes that a living thing goes through from the start to the end of its life. Possibly the most important part of every life cycle is reproduction, which is responsible for creating new life. Bird eggs are <u>fertilised</u> while they are still inside the female bird and only develop their hard shell after the fertilisation process is complete.

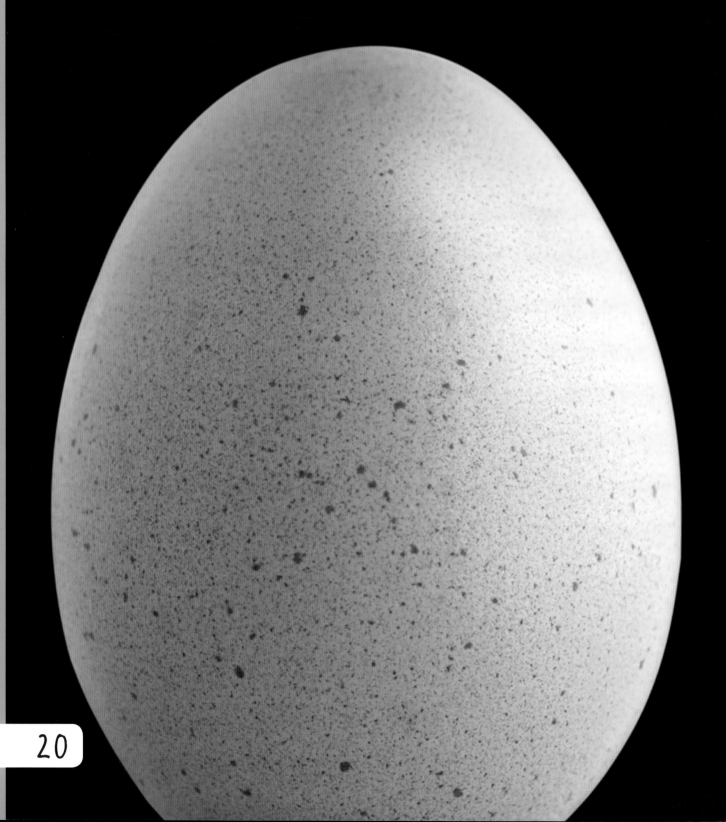

MATING RITUALS

Male birds often have special ways to impress female birds so that they will let them fertilise their eggs.

These are called mating rituals and they are often unique to a single species of bird.

Greater bird-of-paradise

The males in a special group of birds, known as birds-of-paradise, have some of the most amazing mating rituals in all of the animal kingdom. The males have very colourful <u>plumages</u> on various parts of their bodies, which they show off in spectacular displays in order to attract females.

LIFE CYCLE OF A PARROT

Parrots start their lives inside an egg. A baby parrot will use its beak to break its way out of the egg. Birds that have just broken out of their eggs are called hatchlings.

Female adult parrots lay their eggs in the hollows of trees after they have been fertilised by a male. The parents will keep the eggs warm until they hatch by sitting on them and covering them with leaves and twigs. This is called incubating.

Parrot hatchlings are blind and have no feathers when they are born. They rely on their parents to <u>regurgitate</u> food for them and to protect them from predators. A hatchling usually believes that the first living thing it sees is its mother and it will immediately form a strong bond with them. This is called imprinting.

Once the parrot hatchling is stronger and has grown feathers, it is called a fledgling. Fledglings have fluffy feathers that fall out to be replaced by stronger feathers. When a parrot fledgling has grown its stronger feathers, known as flight feathers, it is considered an adult.

EXTREME BIRDS

Some birds have developed extreme habits or skills that help them to survive.

ARCTIC TERN

The Arctic tern has the longest <u>migration</u> of any animal on the planet. Every winter it flies from its <u>breeding grounds</u> in the Arctic to the warmer climates in Antarctica, then six months later it returns back to the Arctic. This means that the Arctic tern flies around 71,000 kilometres every year.

Arctic tern

Size:
35 cm long

Home:
Arctic regions

Diet:
Small fish

24

HUMMINGBIRD

Hummingbirds are able to go backwards or hover in the same place when they fly, almost like they are floating. They are able to do this because their wings flap up to 4,200 times per minute.

Flapping their wings so fast uses a lot of energy and means that a hummingbird can <u>starve</u> in only a few hours. Because of this, hummingbirds often eat twice their own bodyweight in a single day.

Hummingbird

Size:
5 cm – 13 cm long

Home:
North America, South America and the Caribbean

Diet:
Nectar

PEREGRINE FALCON

Peregrine falcons are the fastest predators on the planet and can swoop down on prey at speeds of up to 320 kph. Their eyesight is 12 times better than a human's, which means that they can spot prey from eight kilometres away. Once they find a target, peregrine falcons hold their wings close to their bodies and dive at their prey. Peregrine falcons do not slow down or use their talons to kill. Instead, they smash into their prey at full speed!

Peregrine falcon

Size:
50 cm long

Home:
Everywhere except extremely cold regions

Diet:
Medium-sized birds

EMPEROR PENGUIN

Lots of different birds can swim but none can swim as well as the emperor penguin. Like other penguins, the emperor penguin has developed wings and feet that are brilliant at pushing the bird through the water. However, the emperor penguin is special in that it can dive over 450 metres deep. That's more than the height of the Empire State Building and seven times deeper than most other penguins can dive.

Emperor penguin

Size:
120 cm tall

Home:
Antarctica

Diet:
Fish

BIRDS UNDER THREAT

Lots of the birds that you have seen in this book are in danger of becoming <u>extinct</u>. One problem facing these animals is <u>global warming</u>. This could cause the habitats of many birds to disappear, making it hard for them to survive. Global warming could cause the ice that penguins live on to melt and the areas where raptors live and hunt to become dry and desert-like, making it difficult for these birds to survive and find food.

Electricity and other types of energy are made by burning fossil fuels, which are substances that take millions of years to form naturally. When we burn these fossil fuels, certain gases are released into the atmosphere that make it difficult for heat to leave the planet. This is what is causing global warming – but you can help to stop it!

By using less electricity and recycling as much as possible, you can help to save lots of animals from becoming extinct.

Try these energy-saving tips:

- Turn off all lights and electrical devices when you're not using them.

- Cycle or walk as much as possible.

- Take all of your paper and plastic waste to a recycling centre.

FIND OUT MORE

BOOKS

Birds (Living Things & Their Habitats) by Grace Jones

(BookLife, 2016)

Animal Classification (Discover & Learn) by Steffi Cavell-Clarke

(BookLife, 2017)

WEBSITES

WWF
www.wwf.org.uk

On this website you can follow links to information on all sorts of endangered animals, as well as find out what WWF is doing to save animals all over the world.

National Geographic
www.nationalgeographic.com/animals/birds

Find out about different birds, their natural habitats and the threats they face.

GLOSSARY

adapted	changed over time to suit an environment
breeding grounds	the places where animals go to reproduce and raise their young
extinct	when there are no living members of a species left
fertilised	caused an egg to have developed into a new living thing
global warming	the slow rise of the Earth's temperature, in part caused by the burning of fossil fuels
habitat	the natural home or environment of a living thing
lift	an upward force that makes birds and aeroplanes fly
magnetic field	a protective force around the world that some animals can sense
migration	the seasonal movement of animals from one area to another
organs	parts of an animal that have specific, important jobs
oxygen	a gas that all animals need to breathe in order to stay alive
plumages	the collective name for birds' feathers
regurgitate	to bring up swallowed food to feed young
species	a group of very similar animals that are capable of producing young together
starve	to suffer or even die from not eating or drinking enough
traits	qualities or characteristics
unique	unlike anything else
vertebrate	an animal that has a backbone
wingspan	the distance between the tip of each wing when they are fully stretched out

INDEX